10

of the

Best

Parthian
The Old Surgery
Napier Street
Cardigan
SA43 1ED

www.parthianbooks.co.uk

First published in 2011
© Siôn Tomos Owen, Michael Oliver,
Anna Lewis, Alan Kellermann, and Mab Jones
All Rights Reserved

ISBN 978 1906998 45 5

Editor: Lucy Llewellyn
Design & typesetting by Lucy Llewellyn
Printed and bound by Dinefwr Press, Llandybïe

The publisher acknowledges the financial support of the
Welsh Books Council.

British Library Cataloguing in Publication Data

A cataloguing record for this book is available from the
British Library

10

of the

Best

Selected Poetry
by

Siôn Tomos Owen
M. A. Oliver
Anna Lewis
Alan Kellermann
Mab Jones

Contents

Alan Kellermann

Mab Jones

Siôn Tomos Owen

Recycle

A great fear of mine
Is to live forever.
Thanks to divinity,
That ethos and morality
Driven into me,
I'm meant to be grateful;
If I queue correctly, quietly and with no fuss,
I'm allowed in,
To live (mark II)
Forever.

But if I gratefully decline,
'No thank you',
And step out of line
I'm irrefutably out of options.
Out on a limb.
Out or in?
Out and down.
Down the shoot.
The trap door under my feet,
Into the heat.

Enter free will
And my options are 'forked'.
This metaphor alone
Proves
If I'm awkward through choice,
I pay if I stray

From the designated path,
Which turns steep
If I'm no sheep.
Hell hath no fury
Like the devout jury.
If you're out, surely
You've no right to return?
BELIEVE or BURN
And take care as you alight.

But what if I stay?

No pleasure.
No pain.
I merely
Remain.
Again and again.
I get to experience
both sides of every fence.
From silver spoon
To meagre bowl.

Every colour, creed, sex.
Nothing complex.
A reinserted soul.
Brand new immersion
In a brew of daughters and sons.
Every time.
No waiting in line,
Anxious, agitated.
Emancipated from any afterlife.
Simply;

Birth
     Living
          Death

               (a slight lull)

Then recycled
As a glass half full.

October 21st 1966: Today's Headlines

A
Landslide,
Like all news,
Travels quickly
Unfortunately
One hundred forty-four
Soft, screaming, struggling voices
Unavailable for comment
Gave a definite answer
To the coal board today
Concerning the tip
Tow'ring above
Their Local
Prim'ry
School.

The Bwlch

A Goliath, guarding.
Huge in hues of hay and gold and stone.
Shimmering from a fold,
A trickle tumbles
To greet the greater rushing force.
The forest framing its path.
Regimental firs amongst the rugged fern
Pose proud as the gorse,
Prickly and persistent,
Thrusts its yellow bud to the sun.
Precariously pretty from the ledge,
Daffodils, heads lifted,
Cling to lips of light.

Soon seasons will stain these black marks
From firesnatched schoolboys' stunts
Emblazoned across the crest,
But beaten each time by allowing spring
To bring the resistance in green shoots,
Reborn through the bronze bereaved.

A steadfast ram postures
The single creeping car
Struggling
Along the coiling mountain road.
A single bead of sweat
Descending
Over the brow.

A shawl of shadow
Drapes its way across the basin,
Easing its way over curve and cliff.
With dip and weave,
Nests are featherbound and filled.
Songs are settled, sweetly.
Daylight dims with scattered braying
Closing to the mantle.
Welcoming and framed as postcards
Of the terraced lives below.
Unknowing and unrelenting,
The Bwlch still stands,
The valley's beauty to bestow.

Worried they'll get in
(after 5am May 7th 2010)

If something was broken
You'd try to fix it,
To patch it.
But I promise you
Wouldn't want to Margaret Thatch it
Again.
Cause those who were brought up politically correct
Won't remember or conveniently forget
That the last time it happened
The class war was born at the helm,
The fabric of society torn.
The embroidered hem
Unravelled to reveal
Mass unemployment
That wasn't their problem,
Though it WAS Them, they, her, she caused it.
Ripping out souls to heat their second homes
Cause coal was out, picketing.
So it's sickening to think
That these economic amnesiacs
Will allow a second attack
To come down like an Eton of bricks,
That you can't use to rebuild.
And it'll be too late
Once that mistaken vote is cast,
When her regenerated sirs and snobs
Rob those who never proposed to do a thing
That will benefit the needy,

The ones who still remember the iron lady's tightened
purse
Bulging from Robin Hood in reverse.
Hearing the jangling prospects in their pockets,
Replacing corporate plugs on sockets
And pulling
The trigger on this great big gun.
Run rabbit run rabbit run run run
From this starting pistol
That begins the marathon,
And we're all running against the grain.
Remaining down here,
Cause they're all above us.
We're no longer owed anything.
We owe it all.
They own it all and we have to run it.
One Big Society
Actually run by you and me, us and we?
By anyone other than that cunt
In the tree-lined suburbs of the city,
(Cause it's always the city.)
Constituencies are beef
And each party must pound it
till it's flat and handy to keep in the pantry.
Till they bring it out to feed
The poor knocking on the door
To make the beggars think
'This Number Ten is quick to give.'
So line up line up!
Homelessness for hot chow!
Now you've been thrown out of your house
Cause you were lax.

Cause you weren't married to your spouse.
You'd pay less tax
If you'd popped the question,
Tied the knot and bought a cot.
Cause it's families first,
And while the rest of us are gasping from thirst,
Drinking our troubles away,
Wondering where the next pay packet will come from,
If at all.
It's a short call
Before the notice is up on these four walls.
Can't afford the four-bedroom,
Or three-bedroom, two-bedroom,
One room
Or a roof over our heads.
Cause the overheads have been spread
To cover the previously set-up,
Secured, the backed-up,
The overflowing cup
Lifted to their stiff upper lips
As the working classes' grasp slips.
And those on the ladder are back to square one
Without a dice to roll,
While the snakes are moving in.
And since the stakes are too high to even attempt,
Living's turned to life for rent.
Help, we're surrounded!
Extra hounds on the street won't help,
Won't protect us
From the falling pound,
Unless you've stock piled,
Then you're on to Easy Street,

Or Fiscal Drive, Ever Close,
Youave Avenue.
Where you can't be touched.
Where you can pick and choose
Whether to include the outside world
Or shut it out.
Cause even if you want it,
You don't want to pay for it.
You won't stand for it.
But we have to stay for it
And pray for it,
Cause god help anyone
Who isn't already protected
By cast-iron gated communities,
Surrounded by fences
You don't sit on
Unless it's a hedge fund.
Hundreds of thousands of us
Will be left to fight it out amongst ourselves.
After the shelves have been emptied,
The streets will be filled
With remorseful cries,
X's marking the spots on our shattered eyes,
And the hard place has moved in with the rock
Just to get by.

Appointment

She went without me.
Now, holding her emptiness,
She's filled with regret.

Your heart like a broken wing

Your heart,
Like a broken wing,
Will need mending
To keep you from hurting yourself.

He'll hold you close,
As he's always done.
Whispering reminders
Of your love.

Brushing your hair from your neck.
Revealing,
Stroking your cheek,
The bruised anguish,
Kissing your fingers,
Repeating,
The pain,
His fear of losing you,
Like an echo
Bouncing off these four walls.

He lifts your head.
You hold his gaze
As you once did,
Before you ever touched.

He holds your head in his hands
And, once more,
Promises
That he'll never hit you again.

Are you uncomfortable yet?
(have you realised that you're fucked?)

Prepare yourself.
Fisting the gulping anus of industry,
Felching enthusiasms,
And relentlessly whoring the workforce,
Forcing themselves upon the struggling faces.
Putting them in their places,
Shovelling the steaming faeces
Baking in the stomach ovens of tunnels,
Slogging the sinewy, burning muscles,
Muck and mucus mixed
Till silvery sputum
Dribbles from their knackered,
Shattered, shit-stained pain,
Smeared on the walls of the
Brainchildren of the revolution.
Polluting the unionised front,
Fighting to stay upright
While squeezing through the tight twats
Of the fat cats, lying on their backs.
The pleasing secretion filling their pockets
Of multi-million masturbations,
Cumming in the cunt of corporations.
The bulging bollocks of businesses,
The owners,
Bastards born of the blisters
Popping and pissing out the pus

That customers and consumers slurp and lick
The dicks dangling from the buggerers'
Hairy cracks of the whips.
Black eyes and blue-veined
Throbbing, pulsing and subsidising
Glass and steel erections of sky-high phallics
Funded by the fortitude
Of forgotten and mistreated attitudes.
Fingering the upper classes,
Filling the right glasses,
And fucking the masses.
Cause the shit rolls downhill,
From the tips of slate and slag
Till it lands on the plates
Dissipates the bad taste
Cause we're starving,
Gorging and gagging on the produce.
Hypocritically wanking from hand to mouth.
It's hard to swallow,
But
We welcome it with open arms,
Open legs,
Arses in the air,
Eager and ready
To deny
That we're all paying for it.

The Long Fortnight

If you can get past the guards,
Who regard your stagnant situation
As an institution with no solution,
Other than to stand in this long line
Shuffling your feet
In the wrong pair of unshined shoes.
Unentitled to any common sense.
They do enough to pay your dues.
Answering your queries in riddles,
Weary if you're fidgeting,
Guilt written on your furious faces.
'Get to this place by ten tomorrow.'
'I don't drive, I'll have to borrow for the bus.'
All this fuss for £5.45 an hour.
No wonder there's daily rage.
Fight to survive on minimum wage.
Scowled at cause you're 'scum'.
Don't matter where you've come from.
You've arrived here
Down through the system beggin'
(To get our foot in the door).

You just keep sighing and relying on dole
Until you can't take no more
Of 'sorry we're not taking on'.
So you have to keep signing on and taking less
Unless you mess up the sheet
Or tick the wrong box.
Then they pull the rug from under your feet
And the building blocks come smashing down around
you.
No cash, no progress, no giro, zero, no payment cheques.
Living on loose change to keep the noose from your
necks.
So stay in line, sign, bide your time,
Keep looking, budgeting, scouring the pages
For that opportunity to shine in these dark ages.
Keep up the fight and keep your wallet watertight.
Once more, till week 24, is a long fortnight.

Wet Agnostic

Seasons shift to scatter clouds.
Shroud my shoulders in grumpy brown air.
The heavens open,
to curse my weekend?
To drown my sorrows?
To borrow your grand plan for me
from a fabled ark.
To dampen my spirits?
Then send it down wet.
Hammer it home.
Is this the pitter-patter of payback
cause I stole away?
Like an umbrella ripped
from an unexpecting hand,
left with a soaking handle,
cursing an inanimate object.
Ignorant to the abject insubordination
of the omnipotent.
The masses
intent
on waiting for the Second Coming.
When the reality could be
that he's bumming around puddles,
spouting nonsense and love.
A bearded vagrant,
forsaken again,
now ponderous,
outside an entrance to the underground!

Ignoring the irony.
When it's time for me
to ponder purgatory,
eliminating limbo,
imagine I've winged it
further than expected.
No pearly gates.
No saintly bouncer,
deciding my state of life,
on how many sins I've spent grinning.

Get it over with and be gracious,
good god,
always and amen.
No grey area.
No and/or.
A pillar of salt.
'Thou shalt not have forgot about me.'
Hold on now,
no murder, no marauding, no sodomy.
Just the odd
fuck, bollocks and shit,
a drink,
and I've stared at tits
when I weren't supposed to,
and I once got close to
kissing another bloke.
Choke on that revelation.

That's what I've done.
I've had fun
in a life of sin, grinning.

That's the speech I'd prepare
to meet you face to face
if I cared,
if it were the case,
but it ain't.
They've painted too many different pictures:
a rainbow of religions
deities, idols, saints and scriptures
proclaiming, preaching and teaching,
brimming with cavalier bigotry.
Each one
providing,
from the moment you're born,
shelter from the ever-present storm.
But enjoy the storm!
Thunder and lightning,
very very enlightening,
never strikes the same place twice.
You assume I've been struck
when I wasn't even asked.
No choice,
and I've yet to hear The Voice.
The guiding Light I see
forks the oak,
frees the smokescreen
and washes the argument clean.
Forcing the communal clutch to slip,
which has masked the accusing grip

long enough.
Lending the task
of stoning the doubters and heretics
to be decided by one's own moral compass.
So by sticking to ONE when it's so vast?
And you've condensed it down to words,
The Word,
between two hard covers,
gilded edges,
pledges and confessions.
Creating the impression of
law and order under...
You.

Seven days and a three-act play.
The old, the new and the resurrected
have affected a lot of people
cause it's a hell of a read,
fair play.
Multiple stories,
illustrations too.
But one basic cast?
That's a lot of lines to learn.
One to follow
and none to cross.
A lot of bridges burned.
A lot of pressure on your leading actor.
And a lot of miming.
Paradigmatic ventriliquism.
Very clever.
A bit pessimistic, though.
Don't do this.

Don't do that.
Don't do her.
Definitely don't do him.
Don't kill,
which I agree with,
apart from the odd loophole:
an eye for an eye?
Must be literal,
with a footnote to the use of antiseptic,
otherwise you haven't reflected too much
on the implications
and interpretations
of these proverbs.
If we,
in the midst of life,
are in death,
then our last breath
may heave a sigh of relief.
If you're adamant that peace and freedom
is tied to belief,
then saint or sinner,
veteran or beginner,
each day is a test of faith
to be passed with flying colours.
But I'm constantly thinking
that there's more
than just black or white.
And if I don't shrug this feeling
that if we're perpetually sinking,
then we might as well give up without a fight.

A spiritual autonomy
can be the making of me,
but I am tiny
in villages
towns
cities
countries
continents.
As for planets?
Phew!
With us on it?
A speck
amongst specks
and as a dot in space?

....   !   ....

It's a big place.
A bit sparse
for this tiny story in time,
don't you think?

As to the rain.
And this story of mine?
Blink and you'll miss it.
But c'mon,
I've worked hard all week.
So if you want to make a believer out of me,
send some sun
to the back garden of number 23
'till Thursday,
cause I'm working Easter weekend.

25

Chips Are Wrapped in Yesterday's News

For spraying 'wanker' on the headmaster's BMW,
He went out with a bang.
Fizzled into the annals of schoolboy infamy.
Nobody missed him,
Least of all me.
But his mother's dirty looks
Suggested I led him astray.
Mine told her he was a bad egg from the start.

A year later he was running down the aisle of the train,
Wearing a green jumpsuit,
'Army cadets' in yellow on the back.
Got off
At the stop for the barracks.

I saw him years later
At the chippy,
Through the racist spider web-cracked window.
He spoke as the dark, Middle Eastern-looking man
Sharpened his skewers behind the counter.

He was older, looked more like a man.
He'd learnt to stand to attention.

His pursuit of cool had taken him all the way to Iraq.
Showed the man a corner-creased picture.
A dusty yellow horizon behind him.

He told the man all about his guns.
Best time of his life,
Running round a desert.

He ordered,
'Good old British fish and chips'.
Takeaway.

'Last takeaway for a while.'

As he left the shop, he nodded at me,
Before heading in the opposite direction.

I didn't know him well enough to hear it word of mouth.
I was told of his death
By a grease-covered eulogy
In a cold bag of chips.

Tonight,
I saw him for the last time.
In the chippy,
Posing proudly in his uniform.
Amidst my battered sausage,
Stained in soggy monochrome,
He stared at me with half a headline.
His soldier's accolade smeared in my hands.

M. A. Oliver

How Many Harlequins?

At the beginning of our affair
She led me to her apartment,
The one I later learned
Had been borrowed from a friend
With hazy permission.

Pointing at the wall –
Specifically, a print of
Guernica – she asked
'How many harlequins can you see?'
Confident her knowledge of art
Was greater than mine.

Indeed, I did not know the required answer
And so remained mute
To avoid revealing my ignorance.

Instead I turned to look
Deep into the masterpiece
That was her eyes,
Not seeing a single harlequin
When I should have seen many.

Collected Sayings by American Tourists

(On visiting Caerphilly Castle)

Gosh, that castle must be like a hundred years old. Can you imagine? Everything here is just so old. It's so bizarre.

(On visiting Cardiff Castle)

Gosh this castle is like a hundred years old. It's so hard to imagine how they built this. I mean, they didn't have trucks then did they? It's so bizarre.

(In London on September 11th, an hour after the Twin Towers had been struck)

How could someone do this? I mean how? What were they thinking? Why? Why would anybody do this? We've never hurt anybody.

(Outside St Davids Hall on St David's Day)

This country is so cute. You got dragons and love spoons, and even some of the road signs are in Elvish. It's just like being in *The Lord of the Rings*. I had no idea England was like this.

Hedgehog

A former lover
Once nicknamed me Hedgehog,
Something to do with my spiked hair
And apparent slowness.
How many times have I been asked by friends
'If you were an animal
Which one would you be?'
Never being able to see
Which creature I was like.
How did she get it just so right?
Though I don't think she knew
My constant longing for hibernation,
Or how many times
I had come close to casually walking
In front of a moving car at first light.

Don't Mention Rosie

This didn't used to be just a kitchen,
Just a house.
It was here I saw my children grow;
Each moment I remember,
Just about.

Now there is only silence,
The hum of the fridge at night,
Rattle of washing machine by day,
And the clock, a wedding present,
Which has always stopped at
Odd times.

Silence. Heavy and long
With occasional phone call interruptions,
Which no doubt will eventually
Diminish;
Like old Rosie,
Each bark led to finish.

Was it all a dream?
'Was it all a dream?' I ask out loud,
At the fridge,
At the washing machine,
On the phone, in my head,
And always when I lay in bed.

A family raised and what is there to show?

Children,

Far away now.

And in the garden

Rosie's bones.

Men's Room Etiquette

Entering the men's room is a more complex and stressful event than women realise. Complete with its own rules of engagement, it is or can be a series of highly calculated footsteps and manoeuvres, more so than any form of dance anywhere in the world. This is the men's room etiquette.

On entering the room, if the urinals are empty, take the furthest left (like taking the backseat of the bus, you have to leave room for everyone and make sure there are plenty of options other than right next to you). If the room has one person in it, and he is far left, take the furthest right. However, if this is the low down one for kids, it's perfectly acceptable to take the one next to it. If you have only five urinals or less, and when you enter, some guy has taken the centre one, be careful. He is either drunk, way too confident, or he's on the look out for something (wandering eye syndrome); in this circumstance if there is a cubicle, there is no shame in taking it. If there is no cubicle then you must use the shielding hands technique. This may seem to others (if they are looking) that you have something to hide, but it's perfectly acceptable (especially around those with wandering eye syndrome). If you cannot pee at urinals and have to use the cubicle (cannot pee next to fellas syndrome), this is fine. If you find all the cubicles are full, it is acceptable to wait, so long as you keep your eyes down, cough rough, manly coughs and pull a frustrated, somewhat angry face (like you have turtling head syndrome). There are many men that cannot use the urinal, and they have many reasons for this. Most of them you will find have come out of a tough relationship with a woman and have lost their confidence a bit, or they are simply overly cautious against those men who 'take the other bus'. As long as 'cubicle only men' do not ever look over your shoulder, they should be tolerated. Talking in the men's room is strictly forbidden. Even if your mates are there, it is forbidden. The only time it isn't forbidden is when you are clearly talking to a mate who is taking a shit in a cubicle and fancies a quick chat while you are at the urinal (there is a wall between you, so this is fine). Talking to anyone other than a mate who isn't emptying his bowels in the confines of a cubicle is just wrong. Nobody wants to talk to you. Nobody cares how drunk you are or how well or unwell your night is going. Nobody wants to be asked how their night is going either. You're there to undertake the delicate task of draining the lizard remember, nothing else.

Once you have finished draining the lizard, removing yourself from the urinal zone is basically like reversing a big truck out of an alley, you keep looking behind you – never forward, left, or right. Your only concern now is the way out, or the taps if you're that way inclined. Once you have zipped up, about-turn and get those eyes on the taps, the door, the floor towards the door, or the mirror. If someone is entering as you are leaving, it is his job to keep the door open for you, even if he was just stepping in. You do not want to be seen standing at the door, holding it open for some random guy; why would you linger? The man at the door will understand this, and if he's an impatient bastard then it's perfectly acceptable to use the shoulder when you cross paths. He should know, as all men know, it's wrong to spend any more time than you need in the men's room. You're there to get a job done. Get it done and get out. Nobody wants to be known as 'that guy who takes too long in there'. As long as you obey these few basic rules, nothing bad will happen to you. Remember, the men's room is the only safe haven left (it used to be the entire pub), you should feel confident, safe and comfortable (not too comfortable); enjoy your piss, take your time (not too much time) and leave that room ready to take on your next pint.

Peace Crane

I knew a man who told me this story:

He was once in an airport waiting room,
En route to New Zealand,
All the other people en route to a place,
Waiting,
Perfectly spaced.

A Japanese man sat next to
Our average white Joe of this poem,
Who immediately became worried
He'd want to practise his English on him.

Though this was not the case.
The man from Japan sat patiently and
Systematically,
Passionately,
Created a remarkable crane in origami,
Which only average white Joe could see.

On completion he handed the crane to Joe
And explained that he was
From Hiroshima, and
At this time, every year,
People come from beyond
To Hiroshima
To remember, and to learn
From those that stayed together,
And those who were burned.

The cranes get passed to strangers
In remembrance of hidden dangers,
Even en route to another place,
Passed dangers remembered
And remembered with grace.

Though our Joe, to you unknown,
Told me in his own way
Of that day,
When he happened to be there
Talking to the man
From Japan.

And recalled
How this man of East and Afar
Shaped not only a crane of peace,
But also a ninja star.

Though Joe couldn't produce any crane today
Because it got lost along the way,
He assured me
The star of aggression

Remains

40 pence or 3 for a pound

Beneath the hanging baskets
And northern slate facades,
Beyond the peacocked gardens
And rhyming couplet bards,
Many glasses broken
Into many sabre shards,
Politicians deal with people
Like gamblers deal with cards;
Foreign trafficked women
Are fucked in midnight crawling cars;
Beer-bellied brain-dead
Are brained in local bars.

Picture-perfect postcards
Paint this city like a palace,
Failing to betray the sense
Of hidden, seething malice.

(IF)

And if they ask
Just let them know
I've gone to watch
The river flow.

They might
        Want to know   why

My wallet and keys
        Are left inside

Why all I owned is left behind

And all my clothes
Are still in rows.

Just let them know
I had to go,

I've gone to watch the river flow.

I Took a Trip to the Job Centre

I took a trip to the job centre owing to the fact I had very little money, no way of making any, and like everyone else I too need a means to an end. They have these machines you can browse jobs on. You have to type in your criteria first, so I entered 'unskilled, minimum wage'. The first job that came on screen was a request for a sandwich artist. Well, I can make a sandwich, but whether I can make them artistically is another matter. My sandwiches have always looked appetising but not artistic. So I touched the screen to see what the next job was. Job number two was a request for a sandwich technician. I have my maths and technology GCSEs but I wasn't sure I knew if I could apply them; I did after all only get a C in maths, and the role of sandwich technician sounded rather important. I reasoned that they probably made sandwiches for NASA and the amount of salad had to be directionally proportional to the amount of meat, to be consumed in zero gravity, and if the sandwiches weren't made with absolute precision, we'd have astronauts spontaneously combusting in space. I did not like the idea of such responsibility, so I didn't apply for that job either. Not getting anywhere fast I decided to try applying for jobs with different criteria, so I typed in 'skilled work, maximum wage'. What came up was a request for Welsh Interior Minister for allocating funds to postgraduate scientific research projects.

I remember reading in the paper about a rather

expensive research project on why cornflakes go soggy in milk, in which the results were inconclusive. Now, having been out of work for some time, I had eaten many a bowl of cornflakes and in my frustration at my very singular diet had become accustomed to watching them go soggy in milk. I reasoned that I could probably consider myself an expert in the field of soggy cornflakes, and if I were to take the role of Welsh Interior Minister for allocating funds to postgraduate scientific research projects, I could allocate all the funds to myself, solving both my financial problems and the great existential soggy cornflake crisis. They might even award me the Nobel Prize. So I applied for the job.

I am still waiting.

Eastern Philosophy

Eastern philosophy proclaims
The path of enlightenment
Is to know thyself.

I know myself.
This is precisely
My problem.

Anna Lewis

Penelope

The ancient Britons never did it for me –
their mudded veg and dowdy wattle-and-daub,
accents furling up into our own –

but the Greeks ran me through like a virus:
Daphne skirted the tripwires of my bronchioli,
the Minotaur hoofed at each turn of my gut
and Odysseus wrested his oars down my arteries,
winier, blacker, than any Greek sea.

Their scandals distracted me;
I feared turning bad, as a pear does,
from the core to the skin

and I wished for it,
biting my neatly filed nails at the front of the class,
swinging, swinging my legs from the stool,

as I waited to be re-made by love,
to understand what made the Minotaur steam in his cave,
why Apollo pounded for miles after Daphne,
what made Odysseus flounder

for so long with Circe, Penelope fretting
at some other harbour
baring herself, day after day,
to the scrape of each empty incoming tide.

Lesson

'Alas, poor Yorick,' said Peter as he knelt, and attempted
to fit his hand round the skull's grey bulb –
but at its back, the bone had fused to the rock,

so Peter rested his hand like a doctor feeling for fever,
his little finger draping the nooks of its eyes.
Miss Harrow pulled us back, drew her cane, tick-tick,

over the ribs and the pelvis, tapped each leg bone
and arm bone in turn. Lower down the damp beach,
waves peeled from another oddly lumped slab.

The diagnosis was made by Miss Steele at the
                                    schoolhouse:
in Krakatoa's wreck, the poor souls had stuck
to the hardening lava and floated, become pumice stone,

flotsam, washed up on our Zanzibar a year after.
From Sumatra, most likely, where in a moment
the whole air had gone hot, and an ash-black wind

had swung through windows and doors. We nodded,
watched our old Mr Bones spin and beam on his strings.
'Say a prayer for them, boys,' said Miss Harrow.

Peter read: 'I will never forget you; I have held you
in the palm of my hand. Isaiah 49: 15–16.'
In the East Indies, we had heard, they thought that Allah

was angry, that one mouth after another blamed the
                                                    Dutch.
'No,' said Miss Steele, 'God did not desert them.
From Hell He has delivered them here, cool, to us.'

Everything You Knew

Your Tokyo apartment was
flawless, or so you made it sound:
brisk walls, a kitchen that could scarcely

be entered with unshaded eyes,
and you, sifting your negatives
and prints on the floorboards,

monochrome cheekbones and
clavicles shaving your fingers –
those salt-white skins –

those tar-like lips.
In the Manchester halls
where we met, you seemed

agitated by shadows, sipping
at slim cigarettes, as though
trying to smoke without sound.

Sometimes you went out
with Brazilian friends, flared
hair and skirts, an Amazon of

colour in their make-up and
clothes – a Mitsubishi or two,
which did nothing, you said,

and one time you brought home
a slush-skinned boy,
limp hair and tepid eyes;

you hunched at the table in the
blank morning light, smoking,
quieter even than before.

You didn't take pictures here:
in the one that I took, you grin
wildly, anxious to please,

anxious at finding yourself
on the other side of the lens,
of everything you knew.

Breath

Our mother calls it ozone: the green sour breath
that hefts up from the bay, rising from salt,
heaped seaweed, trapped fronds of water.

We stalk from rock to rock –
the weed's wet blisters pop beneath our feet,
and we hang our shadows from our shoulders,

crouch, wait. Wait, then swiftly dip –
our buckets squirm with crabs,
broad-footed beetles, ghostly shrimp.

Our shadows shrink. We tip the swimming things
back to their niches, lift our weed-stuffed buckets
to our faces, and breathe in. Inside the car,
with windows closed, it smells of seafront evenings.

After dark, craneflies tatter the walls of our strange
bedroom. Lace scuds white at the window;
tight ferns and night-flowers, colourless,

unwind their necks around the edges of the garden.
You sleep; the craneflies sleep; by the chest of drawers
our buckets squeak and sigh: faint voices
seep into the room like steam, and dissipate.

The Cord

Six poems from the Mabinogion

i
Arawn's Wife

Suddenly, the nights have changed shape.
The first is long and narrow.
Arawn's wife lies on her side,
stares at the back of her husband's head,
measures the spool of his breath.
An hour passes before she sleeps.

Weeks. The nights tighten:
she kicks at her husband's legs,
stammers his back with her hands,
asks his shoulders again and again
why he has changed.
He ignores her; she cries; her days
are stiff with tiredness. She is taut
with her maids, suspects each in turn.

Months, and the nights draw back.
Moonlight is usual now,
soothes her, like distant music.
She trails the curve of his neck
with quiet fingers.
She cries a little, still,
her body weighed down

with useless organs, with such
pointless and bulky cushions of flesh.

The third season slows to the fourth
and the nights are shallower,
like young waves in a retreating tide.
He tells her his dreams in the
mornings; she tells him hers.

Arawn, a king of the Otherworld, trades place and form with
another man, Pwyll. Arawn does not tell his wife.

ii
Teyrnon's Wife

If you are lying, I can't tell.
You sleep deeply, eat heftily;
each pocket of your body still
clasps its old scent.
                              In privacy,
your fingers drawl my back,
their pace and pressure unchanged –
and your lips buffing my shoulder,
the rough of your knee parting mine:
all as it should be.

But I watch the child mimicking
you in the field; the narrow window,
the sun's low sweep. His shadow
shakes into yours, keeps to its line.
That night, when you knocked at
my room – 'I have found a boy,
if you will keep him' –

something came loose in me.
Now, you say, you have an idea
of his mother: the Lady who waits
by the horse-block at her husband's gate,
and carries strangers to court, in penance
for losing their child.

You don't invite me there with you.
I would have ridden her, the mare,
and spurred her for good measure;

only, I never want to know
the saddle of her hips under mine,
the charge of her breasts against my hands.

Teyrnon finds and raises an abandoned child, probably the
missing son of Pwyll and his wife Rhiannon, at whose court
Teyrnon once served.

iii
Manawydan

I have worn her down:
I mused for hours on outsoles and uppers,
pondered over this leather or that –

I made her test the tread of my shoes,
chased and counted her footsteps, and now
I don't know where she walks; my stitches won't hold.

It hurts to think of the flex of her feet as she moves:
the arches hitching and flattening,
the flicker of those birch-bones, like shadows under
the skin.

I have heard that in some fantastic, faraway land,
they break and fold the feet of small girls
and bind them in silk,
making their women exquisite, and lame;

and I dream of Rhiannon,
bandaged and bloodied, and twisting
on a strange forest floor, as cherry blossom falls
and gathers in drifts, like red snow.

Manawydan takes work as a shoemaker. His wife Rhiannon,
Pwyll's widow, vanishes.

59

iv
Llwyd's Wife

For weeks, I have worried
that you will be born a timid,
snuffling thing, fraught with dreams

of wheat fields high as forests,
of giants looming towards you
with gaping hands.

You drift at the end of my blood:
every picture, each word,
taps like a code down this cord

to you poised,
wide-eyed in the dark as a sentry
and ready. Receiving, receiving.

Llwyd's pregnant wife is turned into a mouse. She is captured
by Manawydan, and narrowly survives.

Aranrhod

One comes with the other;
you may call either one by each name.
Wolf: boar. One held down the girl
while the other held shut the door.

Boar: stag. I left both of my brothers,
but one followed me to my castle's gate.
Uncle: father. He holds up the child
as a priest lifts bread and wine.

Son: nephew. I do not recognise him.
A gawping boy, vacant
as a flower's splayed face.

Aranrhod refuses to acknowledge her illegitimate son, who
was raised by her brother Gwydion. Gwydion and his brother
were, previously, turned into animals as punishment for rape.

vi
Goewin

He has made his peace with my husband.
They embrace in our hallway,
and I sit with them both at table.

He is here for a favour: a bride for his son,
and the men select oak flower, meadowsweet, broom.
They take turns to pluck, thread and twist
until their hands slide with juices,

until, at last light,
they coax a girl from carpels and stamens,
from sepals and slender petals.

She stands naked between them,
skin sticky with sap,
breasts still swelling from her chest.
Their tips slowly firm and ripen, dark as fumitory.

Goewin's husband forgives his friend Gwydion for Goewin's
rape.

Alan Kellermann

Poet Crossing[1]

Three masts crucified against an ailing
moon mark our passage through waves
for ages unsplit by curragh or coracle.

Marked men, you and I. We throw talismans
to the sea, wards, trinkets to sate
not what ranges the depths, but what mumbles

under our own currents: every traveller's fear
that his discovery is not what he seeks. You
resettle your hat and lead on, parse

the sky with unsurety, a hierophant reading
scattered bones plucked from decaying memories.
A gannet on the prow skitters forward, signals

the end. The island hunchbacked
under a great hall, its three doors impossible
enough to keep even memory out. An island

that marks time so we don't have to; remembers
the faces we'll not forget, but gently
surrender. You know well it's a matter of time

before we prowl through that southern door,
become strangers to the sand under our feet; even
the grass we leave behind us a sharper green.

---

1. *Poet Crossing*, Tony Goble, oil on canvas

Sleeping Woman[2]

'They are one – the knowledge and the dream.'
Ambrose Bierce, *The Devil's Dictionary*

I was sailing my sofa – asleep – some
Monday in June
                    the best month
for cushioned seamanship
                         when I woke
to a woman aweather
                     and somewhat worryingly
saw
      owling her with a look toothed
like cracked glass
                    this heron-necked harbinger
glowering down, wings swept aloft
                                  lifted
lorded terminally over her. The look of a carrion-
crow, wilful.

How unaware she was of her still
black stalker – uncut, life-
less, but hardly deceased, a hand
                                 against
her cheek – a ward it seemed, or promise. I
tried to close but couldn't
                            davenport[3] navigation
being tougher than it seems.

               My manoeuvring
was hasty in chase,
           my ship
equipped purely for a nap. Hers, rigged
for a longer rest outran
               with little difficulty,
my craft
        adrift, lost as last night's fantasy.

At last, enfolded in sunset
               she rose
up tomorrow's side of earth, split night
open on a fresh frost – grass
stiff as talons
          shearing through
from some deeper world.

---

2. Tony Goble, pencil on paper
3. davenport – sofa

The Poet Reclining[4]

'this Friday morning, to whoever is cooped up...
to him I come, and without speaking or looking
I arrive and open the door of his prison'
        Pablo Neruda, 'The Poet's Obligation'

Of course it wasn't a sombrero –
only at first glance – but
a coat
        bundled
beneath your head.

I was, admittedly, startled
a bit when you knocked, instead
of ringing the bell like a landlord
or salesman.
                I asked why
you'd come: for an eyeful
of sea, an acre or two of green; should I
deny an elder of my craft the blood-
purple revolution in the evening sky?

Rhossili, then. Through stonewalled
sheepfielded, hillrolling roadways.
From my fledgling Welsh, *araf*, I explained
as if there were need of it, means 'slow'.
Your long nods spelled
                        perfect
in time with the tyres' backbeat

on asphalt; drifted again
out to the hills as if waiting
for realisation come charging over
like Glyndwr's cavalry.

We sat in the last grass closest
to the leap, while the sun groaned
toward the horizon. If a word
would have passed between us,
it could only have been
                              ymwelwr:[5]
me, an outsider in a house I thought
I knew. You, comfortably foreign,
reclined like the gentle dead; for a pillow
your coat, the yellow of straw hats.

---

4. *The Poet Reclining*, oil on board, Marc Chagall
5. *ymwelwr*, Welsh. tourist, visitor

Self-Portrait with Muse[6]

after Nigel Jenkins

At first, *cariad*, I saw you
in the magician's parlour, dusting
wings feathered equal parts smoke
and mirrors. Behind you, afternoon

blue, on which (after its sorcery stripped
us to our nakedest particles) we drew
the curtains. You showed me rare
geometries, *awen*:[7] lines

curved furious, your fingers spidered
down to my brush. To the stroke
and circle and a pallid accent pulled
overlimb through a shadow

ambush, descending one on another
as if night meeting water. Then
having stolen (by sleight
of hand alone) the gods' fire,

we rested. Only moments,
these. Such was it always: adrift
amid myriad fleeting
mirages – some sliver

of thigh, a feather loose
upon the strand. Sometimes I forgot
what magic was, mired
in the purgatory between day-

dream and spark until, for all your mosaic
pieces, you rose from the electric
core of my atoms – wingspread –
in divine cataclysm.

6. *Self-Portrait with Muse*, 1917–18; Marc Chagall, oil on canvas
7. *awen*: Welsh. Muse

Cubist Landscape[8]

My mornings are notes
on someone else's table.
My evenings, bad

               poker
hands shuffled in amongst
them. Afternoons are
a grocery list I keep adding
to, and when I return from
the shops in the rain –
I have only pieces. Not enough
of what I need, less than
I want. I dry them; scatter
them on the pile atop scrambled
memos to myself: 'You know,
by the end, Rita Hayworth
couldn't keep it in order,

either.' It's hard, even, to find
a piece of today without it
being interrupted: when we
met in Brynmill earlier, you
looked as young as when
I learned the lesson of counting
the rings on a tree stump.
Nights are rarer notes,
ever on a scrap already busy –
a train ticket to Tenby, a receipt
for toothpaste – singing
colour through the lumped
days I recognise less, as if
someone's clipped them
further, or torn away their edges.

8. Marc Chagall, 1918, oil on canvas

Companion Stars

Retrograde motion, you might say,
is what the stars insist on
reminding us about our history:
we move forward only by stumbling
through our past.

I've returned just once to that London
hotel, where, by today's one-night stand-
ards, we shared nothing at all.

We drank wine from tumblers, like artistes
shunned proper vessels, smoked Dunhills
mostly naked. You framed yourself
in the window, almost too Paris
for London.

And the moon scribbled orange in puddles
surviving a rain we hadn't noticed.

I still have, among the bones
of a sacrificed life, pictures you took. Half-
drunk, two-thirds tired. Something cosmic
about photography: for a moment,
all an eye sees.

I never told you how I wanted
you on my side of that lens
as it gathers up wayward photons
and unites them for age to yellow gently.

There are celestial bodies like us slinging
around the vast black empty. Companion
stars: furies of dust and fire gathered
into each other's orbits, separated only
by the force that binds them.

Still Life with Wine Glasses

for Ashley

We hung at the bar twisting, a little
too hard, the stems of our wine glasses.

Eight years it's been, and even cancer
couldn't have you. So I knew I'd never

have been strong enough. I haven't
scrubbed out the scuffmarks you circled

with your heel; ground out a full-
stop to a short sentence. On this new

year's doorstep, you gift me snapshots
from a life I'll never see again: lofted beds

on rickety splints, a barroom reeking
of piss, a dodgy condom (dodged a bullet).

So much has changed, you say. We've begun
filling the space between us with clichés,

bridging the void with emptier words. We wear
adulthood like battle decorations: I've sheared

off, made home a continent away. Even
my accent is different now. And you – who

always wanted her mother's apron – feel good,
as you imagined, with each tug on those strings.

It's enough. An hour gone of the new
year, glass empty, your embrace,

warm, reserved for an old friend. *You still
smell the same*, you whisper, and are gone

again. My glass empty; too little left to fill it.

like wallpaper she was

air-plain jetting through
my thoughts i think
i'll have another
beer in mind
that she was so
plain as the nose on her
face it you wouldn't
have a chance with her
skin was pale as pearls of
wisdom teeth tight and normal-
ly i wouldn't think i'd
notice her like wallpaper she
was so unremarkable i
couldn't take my eyes
off we go into the wild
blue jeans and a white button-
up go my eyes along her
length stopping at her
head on my pint

clinging to the side-
long glances i'm giving her
trying to catch her
eye don't believe
in love at first
sight of her featureless
features simple as
the palm of her h-
and-y warhol pragmatism
in the way she was painted to-
get-her i'd need to be
simple as a wrench-
ed away my
eyes wanting to read her skin
like the grain in
wood love to have her
define the rooms
i live in like wallpaper
she was

The Lovers[9]

after 'Waiting', by Yevgeny Yevtushenko

I won't wait for you
                      by the window. When
you come, I'll know it as the latch on memory's
door unclicked, hear your bare heels on the stair-
case, poured into my spaces with the night, with
the rain, all wet hair and leaves left footprint-like
up to my chair where we are love letters folded
into the envelopes of each other; the night
table reddens, envious; dark unshapes us, thickens
evening until there's no room even for shadows,
and your dress, unnecessary, pools blue
at our feet.

---

9. Marc Chagall, 1911–14, oil on canvas

Dry Martini

From 'Stirred: The Martini Poems'

You're sleek
                as a cocktail glass
I'd say
        because
                    my gaze
careering upwards
                    from your feet
needs those two *E*s
                    (long vowel)
to climb all the way
up
      your stem
                  to the lip
where you open
in that consonant
                        crisp
as gin
        and I plunge in
headlong –
a skewered olive
                    drowning
under subtle swells.

Mab Jones

I Am Born
(or, All the World's a Stage!)

My mother broke birth to me,
And there I was:
A silent lump of flesh and blood,
Entwined in afterbirth,
Wearing the placenta as a hat.

And immediately I started
Entertaining the doctors and nurses.
'Burble burble waaah!' I said,
(Which translated to the audience
As a scream)
I am here to entertain you!'

My mother lay quiet on the metal bed.
I had ripped her badly.

I shimmied a blood-red boa
And smiled. But then,
The doctor picked me upside down,
And I hung mid-air like a joker
And I realised:
I'd left something backstage.
But I couldn't remember what.

And then I screamed for real
As the doctor sewed and sealed the
Red curtains I'd rag-tagged through;

And the nurse measured me
With pincers;

And there was no happy father there.
And despite my initial confident
Entrance:

I was filled with stage fright.

Second Form

A schoolgirl who sprouted rather than blossomed;
Who, autumn term, returned with more up top
Than most of her peers, and in games lessons
Drew stares and sneers from the griddle-chested lot.

An object of mirth, subject to derision
Her artichoke breasts and dinosaur thighs,
But boys looked her way more than once in revision,
And the male teachers rulered her with their eyes.

Twelve years old, but belly and bosoms like fruit
On the vine, her unsexed limbs still growing,
Feeling their way into the light: a square root
Alright, her virginal mind not knowing

How those marrow hips distracted, disturbed
(More so, somehow, under the thick grey pleats
Of the uniform skirt). Her body all curves
But she sat in the playground eating boiled sweets,

Or reading and scribbling cartoons at her desk.
A cloud-headed girl despite the earthy weight
Of her new form, as if that female heft
Was unconnected to her mental state:

A butterfly floating above a swede.
A clumsy elephant in class and slow,
But in her work sometimes there was a seed
Quite strange indeed, and if allowed to grow

Might have made, despite her form, a poet.
But as it was, they never let her sow it.
On chalky ground she spilled each acorn word
And works in a launderette now, last I heard.

The Three Coats

So, I inherited these three coats
Of rabbit, mink, and fox.

The first was a pale blonde,
Ankle-length and downy.

The second was a deep brunette,
The colour of roast coffee.

The third was a fulsome red,
Magnificently fiery.

Like three princesses they lived
In the dark of my mother's wardrobe.

Our future selves, we loved to think,
As my sisters and I caressed them.

And some might say that this is
Wrong: to kill an animal for its skin;

Wrong, and even more to long
For them myself – think of the poor things

Dying, lying there just-butchered.
I should respect the lives that were,

Should take these hides, long-hidden,
Out to the woods and bury them.

But more than this I respect my mother,
For I know how she earned the three

(Think of a throat in a huntsman's grip,
The rip of skin as the knife slides in...)

It would be a sin, I think, not to wear
What my mother paid for, skin for skin.

So throw your red paint, if you dare,
The colour of a tongue or a cashbox;

My mother's secrets breathed through furs
Of rabbit, mink, and fox.

Life in an Office

Give me a smiley
Not because it hasn't happened
But because it never will

Give me an emoticon
Emphasis on the final syllable.

Give me that grinning symbol
Like a grotesque hanging
At the end of a sentence

Give me a smiley, go on
Clown it out as clots grow
Fat and fatter
Fistulas in your underdesk legs

Give me a smiley
Its mouth a thumbnail
Deep-bitten into a stressball

Give another smiley
As your request for overtime
Is overlooked

A smiley for that appraisal
A smiley for that reprisal
A smiley that smiles

Until the features gently melt
Into a deaths-head

Stop

Flagging

The fire-breathing dragon now barely breathes at all.
Sometimes you can hear it in the hwup of a flag
Or the fingering whisper of an old poem;
Sometimes you'll catch it in a long and winding cliché
Or high on a lonely platitude.
Sometimes in a scent of music. Sometimes in a farting
                                            echo.

But you have to strain. The sound is weak.
A faint thread in the muffled mist – weak purl
From a throat grown thin as a knitting needle.
Listen hard, but all your ears will grasp
Is the odd, dropped stitch of a sound
That links us now to nothing but a vague
                                    remembrance.

Remembrance: of a red flame on a green hill.
Red for blood and battle, the deep arteries of our
                                            heritage;
Green fresh and wet as a wound. Remembrance
Of the fire-birthed beast, wild and intemperate,
Its back a wall of daggers and its tongue a sword,
And when it roared it was in a voice simultaneously
                                    singeing and singing.
Now the creature this country was lies like a lung
                                            collapsed.
A plastic bag, ripped and tossed: a carrier
Of some wasting sickness. With broken daggers and
                                    blunted sword,

It lies dim in its hollow and rasps its last.
The elemental dragon, once dangerous as an atom,
Sinks and fades like a dying sun, our country's dying
                                                    past.

Beautiful Girl

People supposes that under her clotheses
This beautiful girl has a body like Venus

What no-one knows is that under her clotheses
This beautiful girl has a very large penis

They look at her from top of head down to toeses
They see this great swell of two bosoms like roses
They note her fine boneses and feminine poses
And think: 'what a beautiful girl'

But if she don't shave for a month then her nose is
Choked up with hairs, she is bearded like Moses
And if she uncloses her legs then her hose is
Proof, she's no beautiful girl

But people supposes on clotheses and poses
Their ideas are based on our outer regalia

What the girl knows but will never expose is
The fact that down there she has male genitalia

On external looks people make diagnoses
Their eyes see some things and their mind then
imposes
An idea on which it then somehow closes
And which it will never unfurl

And if this is true, men, then what I propose is
Don't feel obliged to wear doublets and hoses
If you want to oppose this, wear the right clotheses
You can be a beautiful girl

Ever, After

Imagine Snow White with her colours mixed up:
Eyes black as coal and lips white as snow,
Hair red as the rose that blooms in the glass,
That once filled her throat: the colour of stop.
Her bracelets are scars, her necklace a rope
Of clear plastic beads that look just like tears.

Seventeen years but her body's fresh snow
Marked by deep tracks, by the burn of the rope
She pulls to bring the shy vein singing up
Like a river from the arm, to fill the glass
With its red plume, via the needle that tears
At the flesh. She has no power to stop

Using, or being used. They bind her with rope
And sit there like kings, commanding her tears,
Music to them as they move mounts of snow
Through trumpeted notes. They beat her up
And laugh, laugh again, when she begs them to stop.
And after their play, her face in the glass:

Eyes black as kohl from the swift-flowing tears
That only the needle's puncture can stop.
With sharp steel she'll prick the thin vein like rope
And swoon into a blank of television snow,
The static that storms behind the glass
At transmission's end. Turn the volume up:

Silence. How quickly the needle can stop
All sounds, as if she's been laid under glass;
Can, with its cold point, stem the hot tears
And with the same touch slice the slick rope
That binds body and mind. Strings of patched up
Memories, thought threads, buried beneath a snow

Drift. The grim reaper's trickling hourglass
Momentarily still. She'd never wake up
If choice was hers; if she could bring full stop
To this mortal world of blood, sweat and tears
And remain a princess asleep in the snow,
Pulled to her casket by the tight rubber rope.

A fairy-tale fuck-up, she tells snow
White lies sometimes to the glass: that she'll stop,
Soon. A rope that she clings to; that easily tears.

The Ballad of Angharad

Once upon a time there lived a young girl
A princess although she was raised as a pauper
Born into dirt but really a pearl
A diamond, a gem, a blue-blooded daughter
Descended from princes whose reigns are now dead
But of course no one knew that this girl was a
                                            treasure
As a baby the princess was dropped on her head
As she grew men who knew her IQ was low measure
Used the young girl for their own secret pleasure

She put the cum into Cymru all right
A few blokes each day and a few more each night
A Welsh Cinderella who'd let any fella
Try her for size if the payment was right

Carbuncled uncles and toad-featured teachers
Misused Angharad, this young girl so precious
Because she was simple these perverted creatures
Bribed her with Mars Bars and packs of Refreshers
And tho it was seedy, the young girl was greedy
She liked getting sweets in return for her use
Sweets turned to cash as the blokes got more needy
They felt if they paid then it wasn't abuse
Not much, being tight, but it kept the girl loose

She put the cum into Cymru okay
A few blokes each night and a few more each day

A Cardiff born beauty who'd give all her booty
To any old beast who would ask and could pay

She should have grown up into a princess
Instead she was selling herself on the streets
She would undress for a tenner or less
Sixteen but she'd been on a million back seats
Her low IQ gave her a baby-like smile
Which most of her clients found very disarming
The most popular girl on the Riverside mile
She made every customer feel like Prince Charming
Except that she screwed at a rate quite alarming

She put the cum into Cymru its true
There wasn't much else that the poor girl could do
A Celtic Snow White who wasn't quite right
In the head, though in bed she still knew what to do

In stories a princess will often get wed
And live happily ever after
But this one was dropped on her head as I said
Her tale ends in tears not laughter
Pure-bred Angharad, unread, underfed
Caught a disease in some sick fucker's bed
It spread, now she's dead
And she has gone to the hereafter
So, unhappily, you'll never shaft 'er.

This is A Poem

with a title that tumbles into the first line,
headlong, headstrong, with a sense of
entitlement. A trickster poem, its first offence
that thing you think a name. This is a poem
that doesn't wait for you to collect or gather
thoughts; doesn't sit there while you pause,
and then, begin. This is a poem that takes you in,
a sales pitch to itself; that shifts the posts to kick
you into some uncertain goal. But, don't fret.
You don't have to wait 'til the end. You can leave
at any point, grammatical or otherwise.
If this is a poem you really despise then please,
stop reading. Leave. Don't bother with courtesy.
We won't pause, won't even remember because
this is a poem like life, you see.

The End

I was watching television
        When the picture went astray
And there came a strange transmission:
        'The government is sad to say
That there's been a nuclear fission
        In this land we love today
So we've made the swift decision
        To leave you here and go away.
We bring this message, in our wisdom
        Hours later – as you lay
Asleep we were already risen
        And halfway on our holiday.
Yes, there's been a cataclysm
        And yes, we would've liked to stay
But we thought the best thing isn't
        To remain and, like you, pay
The price that radioactivism
        Will wreak in your DNA.
Take heart, dear United Kingdom
        Tho of sunshine there's no ray
(Literally, for the frisson
        Of the fission caused a grey
Mass to mass up, and all vision
        Is, inside a fiery spray,
Lost thanks to this foul emission –
        It rose just like a blown ashtray
Or a sudden apparition)
        We would still like to convey

Our sorrow, and we do envision
        Our return some future day.
Until then, it is our mission
        Still to rule the dear UK
Tho we'll do it from a distant
        Base out near the USA.
T'will be hard, but do not listen
        To what cynics will convey;
It's not time now for suspicion,
        But to face this sad melee
With the guts befits a Briton
        Fighting in a fresh foray.
Challenges there'll be, so kiss 'em,
        Embrace suffering we pray;
Do not stoop to pessimism –
        It's too late now anyway.
Forgive your local politician,
        Think him not a popinjay;
In such times we turn tactician
        And must prevent our own decay
In order to aid your condition:
        Which we'll do from this far bay.
Be of cool, calm disposition
        And try not to feel dismay
If your skin's in poor condition
        With huge blotches on display.
This is fine, in your position,
        And, if you have time, survey
The other people in your vision:
        They're mottled in a similar way.
There might perhaps be a physician
        Who, with poultice, can assay

The pain that this swift demolition
        Of the skin will cause, but they
Cannot cure it; no magician
        Could, so, like a flesh bouquet,
Let each bloody acquisition
        Flourish in a red array.
In short, against our own volition
        We left, but we did not betray
Your trust: we recommend submission,
        Do not make cries of 'foul play'.
We have here some ammunition –
        So before you speak please weigh
Up your verbal composition;
        Every school, house and café,
Has, by a council technician,
        Been fitted with a hidden ray
Device, which picks up with precision
        Every word; so if you sway
A little left of our petition,
        We'll turn your bodies back to clay.
Now, I must make an admission –
        I am late for a soiree.
There will be a fine musician
        And a freshly made soufflé.
I leave you then to your new prison.
        Please don't cry, you'll be okay
As long as you accept tradition:
        Us to rule; you to obey.

The Poets

Siôn Tomos Owen was born and bred in the Rhondda valley, which has fuelled most of his poetry since he was very young. His poems have been published in *Y Gloran*, *Square* magazine, *Nu* and *Nu2*. Siôn's poems have won awards and competitions including runner-up in the Robin Reeves Prize for Young Writers, and he has performed at a number of poetry events including the Hay Literary Festival, Hay Poetry Jamboree and Swansea 24-hour poetry marathon. Siôn studied media and creative writing at Trinity College, Carmarthen and is the lead singer and lyricist for the band The Pine Barons. He aims to write for the people, like a newspaper should, only with more truth.

M. A. Oliver was born in Ely, Cardiff and grew up in a difficult and troubled family which led to an obsession with poetry. Regardless of the menial jobs he has undertaken to pay the bills, he is first and foremost a poet, and has read poetry every single day for the past ten years, focusing mainly on the works of Abse, Larkin, Yevtushenko, L'Anselme and Prévert. His aim in life is to write a poem as catchy and accessible as Jean L'Anselmes poem '1515'.

Anna Lewis was born in 1984. Her poems have been published in magazines including *Agenda*, *New Welsh Review*, *Poetry Wales* and *The Shop*, and she has performed at the Oxford Literary Festival, the Cardiff

BayLit Festival and at the Welsh Assembly. She has won several awards for her poetry, including the Christopher Tower prize, the Foyle Young Poets of the Year award and the Robin Reeves Prize for Young Writers, and is the recipient of a bursary from Academi to work towards her first collection. In 2010 she won the Orange/Harper's Bazaar short story competition. She lives in Cardiff.

Mab Jones is from Ely, Cardiff. As a sufferer of selective mutism, she hardly spoke for a period of eight years, before accidentally attending an Academi open mic and ending up on BBC Radio 4. Since then, she has been a winner in the John Tripp Spoken Poetry Award, the Liverpool Lennon Performance Poetry competition, the Farrago Zoo Awards, and more; headlined most of the major UK spoken word events; represented Wales at the Smithsonian Folklife Festival in Washington DC; worked with WNO, NTW, etc.; and much else besides. She has an MA in English literature, too. www.mabjones.com

Alan Kellermann, born in Wisconsin (USA), is finalising his PhD, an epic poem in two narrative voices, at Swansea University in Wales, where he is on the *Swansea Review* editorial board. Among other publications, his poems have or will have appeared in such periodicals as *Planet*, *New Welsh Review*, *Agenda* and *Poetry Ireland Review*. His work has been anthologised in *Nu* and *Another Country: Haiku Poetry from Wales*.

More poetry from Parthian

  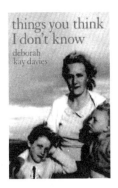

www.parthianbooks.com

Also in the Bright Young Things series

www.brightyoungthings.info